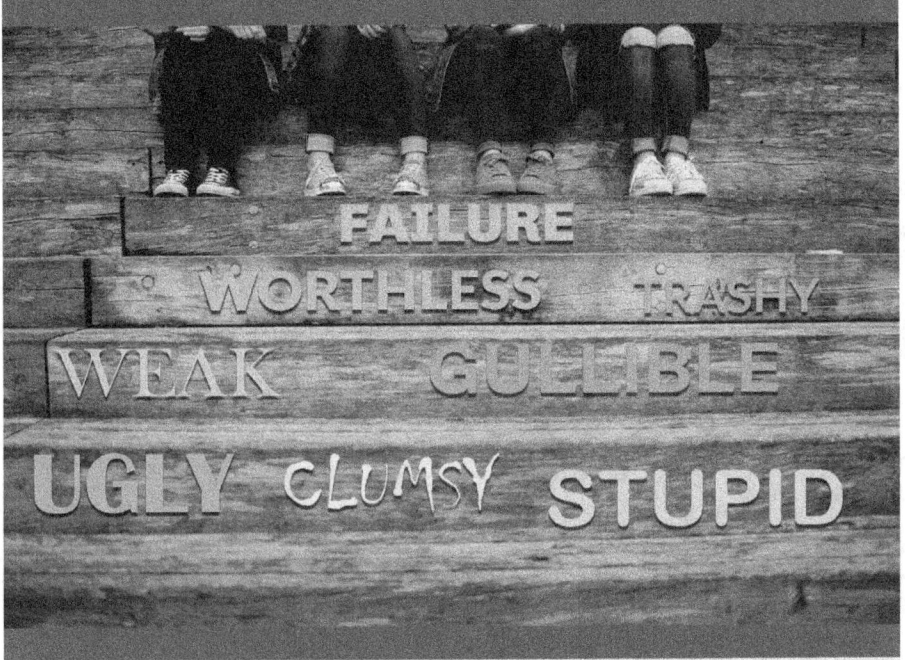

Compiled By:
Tosha R. Dearbone

Tosha R. Dearbone

Turbulence of Self-Esteem
A Young Ladies Journey

Compiled By:
Tosha R. Dearbone

Foreword By:
LaTonya Armstrong

Contributions By:
Ashantra Harris
Dajai Williams
Destiny Walker
Gracie Greene
Havilyn Dawson
Jadah Jones
Jenora Lynn
Jiherra Daniels
Kristian Bell
Latoya Christman
Nykell Lee
Tearini Hubert

Pearly Gates Publishing LLC
INSPIRING CHRISTIAN AUTHORS TO BE AUTHORS

Pearly Gates Publishing, LLC, Houston, Texas

Turbulence of Self-Esteem

Turbulence of Self-Esteem:
A Young Ladies Journey

Copyright © 2019
Tosha R. Dearbone

All Rights Reserved.
No portion of this publication may be reproduced, stored in any electronic system, or transmitted in any form or by any means (electronic, mechanical, photocopy, recording, or otherwise) without written permission from the publisher. Brief quotations may be used in literary reviews.

Print ISBN: 978-1-947445-62-8

Scripture references are used with permission via Zondervan at Biblegateway.com.
Public Domain.

For information and bulk ordering, contact:
Pearly Gates Publishing, LLC
Angela Edwards, CEO
P.O. Box 62287
Houston, TX 77205
BestSeller@PearlyGatesPublishing.com

Tosha R. Dearbone

Dedication

This book is dedicated to every young lady who has ever felt she could not move beyond the challenges in her life, whether they be from within or the outside distractions that come into play. You are *more* than a **CONQUEROR!**

Stay focused and know that if you add the proper principles to gain tunnel vision, you shall **OVERCOME**. Self-esteem is yours to *"Finish the race, complete the work, and get the job done."*
~ **Pastor James Edwards** ~

Tosha Dearbone

Founder
Positive Express

Acknowledgements

When God first gave me this assignment, He gifted me a vision: To bring teen girls together to speak up and speak out about those things that cause turbulence in their lives and affect their self-esteem. Then, I was offered an opportunity to produce this project for free because the "giver" stated, *"This is something I want to do for you."* Well, that did not happen. **BUT GOD!** He instantly said to me, *"I did not gift you an assignment to wait on others to fulfill it!"* So, I picked up my head and refused to allow the enemy to shut down what God had already gifted me to do. To that person who turned her back on me, I say *"Thank you."* Why? Because your "no" helped me remember who the **TRUE** Source is in my life.

To **Mrs. Angela Edwards**, CEO and Chief Editorial Director of Pearly Gates Publishing, LLC: Thank you for helping me see this vision come true. You have been a great asset to my life. I love you for all that you do!

To every **Co-Author** on this project: I'm sending a *BIG* shout-out! I couldn't have done this without **YOU!**

To **LaTonya Armstrong**: Thank you for writing the Foreword. I knew you would capture my vision and run with it. I love you, Sis!

To **Natosha Lovall**: Thank you, Sis, for rocking it with me. You have been that supportive friend through it *ALL*. I love you!

Tosha R. Dearbone

Last, but not least, to my **Children and Granddaughter**: You keep me going and are always there supporting me on my journey. With you, my life is so much better. I love all of you—and don't you *EVER* forget it!

Foreword

In today's society, we have come a long way as it relates to showing our girls what healthy self-esteem should look like. However, some of us women have not crossed that bridge yet ourselves. For some of us, the damaging effects started when we were little girls. Words were spoken to us that caused us to make some bad decisions, all in the name of "validation."

- ❖ *"You're not pretty."*
- ❖ *"You're not smart."*
- ❖ *"You're not worthy to be loved."*

Isn't it great to know that **GOD** affirms us daily, letting us *ALL* know that we are wonderfully and fearfully made by Him? That should mean more to us than society telling us what we should be. We're not only wonderfully and fearfully made; we are God's very own **MASTERPIECES**! Each of us was made exactly how **HE** desired us to be.

Turbulence of Self-Esteem: A Young Ladies Journey was created with the girl in mind who has a secret or story to tell but is too scared to do so because she has been torn down and her "voice" was taken in the process.

This book was also created for girls all over the world whose mothers played favorites *against* them because they are, for example, "the dark-skinned one with coarse hair." Your hair may not be as curly and as long as your sister's, but you're **BEAUTIFUL**! Hold your head up, young ladies! See how great you are — whether you are dark, light, or rainbow-colored. ***YOU ARE GORGEOUS!***

For the girl who has been molested or raped and feels as if her worth was snatched away, this book is for you, too. You're still worthy and loved, Darling!

No matter what it was that crushed your self-esteem, know that **TODAY** — *this very day* — you **CAN** gain back the confidence you once had. There is nothing too hard for **GOD** to heal!

Always remember that you're exactly the way God created you to be. Hold your head up, knowing that you are **more** than enough, Baby Girl! You never have to make choices that reflect anything different.

Love, Peace, and Blessings!

The Turbulence of Self-Esteem Tribe

LaTonya Armstrong

Introduction

"In the midst of the turbulence, we hang onto hope."

~ Lailah Gifty Akita ~

When I was a young girl, I loved reading books. I would work my way through book after book of the *Babysitter's Club* series while imagining that—like the characters—I had it all together. I often daydreamed about walking a day in their shoes and imagined the good times they shared with family and friends was my reality. The characters gained joy from the simplest of things, such as getting together for a babysitting job. The books are very uplifting and encourage the reader to simply enjoy life.

Turbulence of Self-Esteem: A Young Ladies Journey is about 13 young ladies and women who come together to share their overcomer testimonies. While similar in nature, no two stories are alike. Each author walked a "rocky road" full of ups and downs:

- Rejected
- Abandoned
- Mistreated
- Confused
- And many more…

Each instance caused the writers to have their self-esteem severely affected in some way.

Tosha R. Dearbone

"The greater part of our happiness or misery depends on our disposition and not in our circumstances."

~ **Martha Washington** ~

As an overcomer myself, I strongly believe that **YOU** can overcome any obstacle or challenge you may encounter. It's all about the way we see ourselves. We must have a *positive* thought process and be willing to allow others who accept us — even amid our trials and tribulations — to help propel us forward. Many people view self-esteem as only dealing with self-image, but there's **so much more** to it. You will see just what I mean as you connect with the transparent stories shared within of our up and down moments in life. We made the **CHOICE** to get to the root cause.

So, as you read *Turbulence of Self-Esteem: A Young Ladies Journey*, take a moment to pause after each story to capture the essence of what was written just for you. At the end of this book, you will find questions to ponder and answer, as well as quotes to help you overcome any turbulence that may come against you.

Be well! Be blessed! *Be FREE!*

Turbulence of Self-Esteem

Table of Contents

Dedication vi

Acknowledgements vii

Foreword ix

Introduction xi

Tosha Dearbone
    "Pain Did Not Define Me" 1

Ashantra Harris
    "Insecurities" 9

Dajai Williams
    "Young and Afraid" 15

Destiny Walker
    "Overcoming Low Self-Esteem" 23

Gracie Greene
    "I Am Beauty" 31

Havilyn "Greatest 1" Dawson
    "My Testimony" 39

Jadah Jones
    "What I Didn't Know About Me" 49

Je'Nora Lynn
    "H.E.R. – His Eminent Reflection" 57

Jiherra Daniels
    "I'm Not Alone" 65

Kristian Bell
    "There is Beauty in My Teeth" 71

Latoya Christman
    "My Four-Year-Old Self Needed Internal Healing" 77

Tosha R. Dearbone

Nykell Lee
    "From Orphan to Heir" 85

Tearini Hubert
    "I am NOT What They Say I Am" 93

Conclusion 100

Questions and Quotes 103

Appendix 114

Turbulence of Self-Esteem

Tosha Dearbone

"Pain Did Not Define Me"

Tosha R. Dearbone

As I look back on all of the distractions in my life, I smile. I know you are probably thinking, *"How does that equate to having* **turbulence** *in your life?"* Well, allow me a moment to share…

It all started when I was a young girl. I used to have very vivid dreams. I recall on one particular night, I was awakened to seeing and hearing my dad and my mom's guy friend arguing. I thought I was still dreaming. Soon after, a loud sound reverberated throughout the house; it was the sound of a gun being fired. I then saw that my dad had been shot. I remember the ambulance coming and picking him up.

Everything that happened immediately afterward became foggy until some years later (at least I *think* it was some years later).

I remember my mom picking my brother and me up from school early one day to take us to the hospital to see my dad. By the time we arrived, he had already passed away. I sat there crying and upset as I questioned over and over again, **"Why was my dad taken away from me?"** I then began to think about the moments I would never experience with him. One of my last memories of my dad will always be when I visited his home and was molested by my cousin. That's not a good memory to have to bear for a lifetime.

As time went by, I filled the void left by my father's death with the man who is now my stepdad—the same man who shot my father. Shocking, I know! Even though he and my dad had an altercation, I never disliked him for what he had done. Yes, the gunshot wound left my dad requiring a blood transfusion, but the hospital failed to test the blood properly and he contracted HIV—but that nor the gunshot wound are what killed him. Having the virus caused his body to adopt an autoimmune condition which opened up the door to him acquiring pneumonia. He turned deathly ill and passed away from complications associated with the pneumonia. I would often cry for my dad in silence because I never wanted anyone to know I felt abandoned. Plus, I never wanted my stepdad to think I harbored any hatred toward him (which I genuinely didn't). We actually had and **still** have a close bond to this day. I love him as if he were my biological dad. He found value in me and taught me how to drive and walk in my purpose without ever giving up.

Time progressed, and I came into my teen years. I started being interested in boys. Not knowing much about dating, I kind of "winged it." My mom and I didn't have a close relationship as I would have liked it to be, but we made it work. Our relationship was not like that of a lot of my friends where their mothers would sit and talk to them about boys, girly "stuff, or any other thing I may have needed to be successful in life. Instead, we were more like homegirls. We would spend the weekends shopping and going out to eat. Now, don't get me wrong: That was **fun**! Still, I just felt like I was kind of left out when it came to the mother/daughter talks that would have guided me into the young woman I was supposed to become; a girl that was happy, beautiful, fun, caring, and full of life. I didn't feel that way at all because I felt alone, full of anger, abused, suicidal, and full of insecurities.

In my home, there were three brothers and me. I thought all of the attention was focused on them and that they could do no wrong. They had a relationship with our mother for which I yearned. I often heard them talking with my mom as they discussed their lives and shared their experiences. All the while, I was hurting and feeling left out—but I never said anything. I simply felt like I did not fit in. *Now that I think about it, I'm not sure I was supposed to fit in in the first place.* What I **do** know is that I was treated as if they didn't even want me around. I chose to isolate myself from them and basically "make my own way" through life.

Oddly enough, I began to see patterns that disturbed me. My brothers' girlfriends received more attention than I did from my mom. Crazy, right? You might be asking, *"Why do you say that, Tosha?"* Well, I viewed myself as the "Black Sheep" (or castaway) of the family. I had no one to talk to and was verbally abused by names no sister should ever be called. My mom rarely put a stop to my brothers' bad behaviors, so that abuse became my norm. I learned to live with it.

At the age of 16, I asked to move out of our home. I just **KNEW** I would receive some backlash from asking, but my mom agreed! I was living on my own at 16 years old. **WOW!**

Talk about having to grow up fast! I quickly took notice that the abuse I had endured at home filtered over into my dating life. I accepted the guys I met calling me out of my name, hitting on me, and treating me as if they would leave me if I didn't do certain things for and with them. I did not want to be alone, so the abuse continued. That, of course, destroyed my self-esteem and made me feel unworthy. I did not love myself and couldn't understand why no one else did either. Heck, I didn't even know **HOW** to love myself! I was only sixteen!

Turbulence of Self-Esteem

As a direct effect of putting up with the "mess" in those different relationships, I got pregnant—not once, but five times. One of the pregnancies resulted in me having an abortion. I don't believe I had a thorough understanding of what it was; I just did as I was told. After some time, I remember choosing to be by myself for a while because I no longer wanted to feel like I had to accept any man's bad behavior.

I must have looked like a joke to people. I was a young, single mom with four children and none of their fathers around to help me with them. One of my brothers made me feel even worse (or should I say "confused"). He once said to me, *"Nobody is ever going to want you with four kids!"* I felt like trash. Nonetheless, I brushed it off and pushed forward.

In going forward, I found myself in a dark place. I wanted out! I no longer wanted to live. I was still dating different men and searching for the love I longed for, all while thinking, *"Do I want to live or die?"* I attempted to commit suicide twice with pills. Obviously, I was unsuccessful. I suppose God was not ready for me yet! I still had work to do! Getting up daily with four children who looked up to and depended on me alone motivated me to keep going.

I found myself on a hunt, wanting to get to know who **GOD** was. I made it a habit of attending church, reading more of His Word (the Holy Bible), and even watched plenty of religious and uplifting YouTube videos. At that moment, I knew God was doing something **NEW** in my life!

I then became laser-beam focused on a mission to set a better example for my children, better myself, and prove to my family that I was capable of reaching success. I obtained my high school diploma, took some college courses, graduated from Texas School of Business with my Medical Assistant License, graduated from Avalon Medical School with my certification as a Nursing Assistant, and was on my way to becoming a Registered Nurse. I could often hear my stepdad's voice pushing me along:

"Little Baby, you can do it!"

He always did his best to motivate me when no one else would.

As I got older, I started building my relationship with God and began to tap into my purpose in life. For a while, I worked the job of my dreams at Texas Children's Hospital in Houston, Texas. I worked with adolescents who suffered from eating disorders. I would research and pay close attention to their behaviors. Then, something hit me like a ton of bricks: I had yet to address the issues of my own past. I, too, suffered from low self-esteem, rejection, isolation, anxiety, emotional disorder, and a lack of identity. **WOW!** I just **knew** I had to do something to learn to love myself.

Everything seemed cloudy at first, but as I listened to Sarah Jakes' video "Mirror, Mirror," I began to realize that in order to heal, I had to first forgive *myself*. Forgiving myself would allow me to be free from strongholds and the voice of being a victim, and would give me the clarity to let go of it **ALL**.

Moving forward…

In 2014, I was riding in the car with my children when God began to speak to me. I heard Him loudly say, *"You need to be doing something with young girls and teens."* In that instant, I knew my life was about to take a drastic turn.

Turbulence of Self-Esteem

I was led to start my own business of helping girls recognize their self-worth, open up about the situations that they, too, kept buried deep down inside, and begin the process of internal healing. I named my company "Positive Express." What I **DIDN'T** know was that God was being very strategic about getting me to wholeness and total restoration. I, too, was that young girl in a grown woman's body who was broken and in need of internal healing. Every meeting, event, or project was designed to not just help them, but also myself.

When I look in the mirror today, I see a confident, happy, caring, loving, and God-fearing woman who assists young ladies who are reflective of who I once was. I am that generational curse-breaker. I no longer wanted to feel the pain, yet I realized everything that happened to me was to lead me to my purpose: **To become a voice for many.**

My pain did not define me, and neither does yours. Rise, little sis! Love all of you and accept who you are, even when others have counted you out.

Now, ask yourself: *"HOW DO I DEFINE ME?"*

Tosha R. Dearbone

Turbulence of Self-Esteem

Ashantra Harris

"Insecurities"

Tosha R. Dearbone

There was a beautiful 16-year-old African American girl named A'lexis. She was so insecure about herself because of what others said about her. She lived in a very judgmental hometown where the kids bullied those who weren't fortunate enough to have the latest brand-named clothes and shoes.

A'lexis' insecurity issues started when she was in the 5th grade and continued to grow all the way through to her freshman year in high school. People called her "ugly" and told her she would **never** be pretty. So many people spoke those words to her to the point that she began to believe them. When she was in the 6th grade, puberty struck, and her body started to develop. The more she developed, the more the other children teased and taunted her by saying hurtful things. A'lexis would look at herself in the mirror often, telling herself that she *IS* pretty—no matter what others thought. She soon learned how to ignore their negative comments.

Just as she finally got past not accepting the negative things her peers said about her, her **family members** began talking down on her all the time. They, too, said things like, *"You're ugly,"* and *"Nobody will ever like you."* A'lexis believed them because they were the people she actually listened and looked up to. Hearing that she was ugly from her own *parents* hurt her so bad. In front of other family members, she would act happy and keep a smile on her face. Deep down inside, however, she was broken. None of her family members took notice of her brokenness until she broke down in front of them one day by mistake. At the time her breakdown happened, she had been thinking about all of that negative "stuff," and it overwhelmed her.

Turbulence of Self-Esteem

When A'lexis made it to her 7th-grade year, she met a girl named Nicole. The two of them became best friends. Nicole saw the beautiful side of A'lexis and told her often just how beautiful she was. One day, A'lexis found out that Nicole was talking about her behind her back to other students who didn't really like A'lexis because of her looks and how smart she was. Her middle school years were the hardest for her because of all the mean and rude things she heard from people, including her older brothers and cousins.

A'lexis made the basketball team, and the support she got from her dad, uncles, and a few friends made her forget about everything bad that was happening in her life. Shortly after, Nicole began to spread rumors about A'lexis that weren't true, causing even **more** rude comments to come from her peers. When A'lexis joined the step team, she took pleasure in taking her anger out on the floor when she was stepping. Her stepsisters made her feel really good about her stepping skills and always encouraged her with positive energy.

When A'lexis entered the 8th grade, she was very excited about going to a new school because no one talked bad about her there. The other students were kind to her and always complimented her on her looks. She thought nothing about the negative remarks she received in the past at her old schools. The drama had been left behind.

Things were different for her when she was at home, however. It seemed as if at night, those old issues would resurface when she sat alone in her room. She even tried to commit suicide several times but always stopped short of following through because she would get that one positive thought that outweighed all the bad. There were times A'lexis would try to cut herself to numb the pain, but it never worked. The pain remained. One day, she decided to do something different to ease the torment plaguing her mind: drinking alcohol. She quickly realized *that* wasn't a good "look" for her, so she stopped engaging in that behavior.

A'lexis' freshman year finally came. *Yay!* She made more friends than expected…and boys started paying her attention. She, however, was focused on school—until she met Kevin. He was very nice to her and always told her she was beautiful, no matter what anyone else said. Kevin always made her smile when she was sad. He made her so happy, she couldn't do anything but smile whenever she talked to or was with him. The two of them dated for just over a year until she broke up with him.

That same year, she made a new best friend. The difference between the new friend and Nicole was that A'lexis didn't tell her as much about her business. Nicole had scarred her to the point that she concluded she couldn't trust too many females. In addition to her best friend, she did have a few other females she considered "real friends"…ones she was sure wouldn't switch up on her like the ones in her past. Overall, A'lexis had matured very well through the years and stayed out of drama since her 8th-grade year.

In her sophomore year of high school, her list of friends continued to grow. She also had a job and no longer concerned herself with drama and the boys who gave her lots of attention. There was one boy who was kind and sweet to A'lexis who she thought was so adorable. They dated for about four months before she moved to her new school where she made new friends and a new best friend named Connie. She and Connie

Turbulence of Self-Esteem

were very close. She always had A'lexis' back in important situations, especially when people tried to talk about her. Connie didn't know that A'lexis chose to **ignore** all the hatred and negativity she received because she had long ago told herself not to let those things bother her. After all, what they thought wasn't important! It was that train of thought that enabled her to overcome her insecurities in her 10th-grade year. If she hadn't changed her way of thinking, she probably would have committed suicide. She was genuinely grateful for the support of her friends and *some* of her family members who helped her stay strong—a few of her friends were the ones who actually stopped her from killing herself a few times.

When her 11th-grade year arrived, A'lexis was super excited! She planned on taking her junior year very serious because she had been told that year was the most important of her high school career. She had plans on graduating and attending a university so that she could make her parents proud. A'lexis thought it best to stay to herself because even as a junior, negative things were **still** being said about her. However, the difference was that when she used to allow those things to bother her, she didn't allow that to happen any longer. Rude words are just that: ***RUDE.***

****

I understand that as a female, it can be difficult to overcome some things because we are very different from our male counterparts. We are very emotional and tend to take things more seriously, such as being heartbroken or looking different than the "popular girls."

All in all, us girls must stick together and encourage one another. We are **ALL** beautiful, no matter what anyone else says or thinks. We are **strong** and can do **anything** we put our mind to.

I believe that many of our young girls wouldn't have to experience the things A'lexis did if they had someone assuring them that they are loved just as they are. I advise you to start with loving yourself before you accept love from another person you barely know. It's important to do so because that other person could be showing you "fake love." If you learned to love yourself *first*, you would have an easier time distinguishing between real and fake love. Also, learn to ignore negativity before it overtakes your mind. Please don't act like A'lexis and wait so long that you place a higher value on others' opinions over your own.

In conclusion, some insecurities can overtake your mind if you let them be your main focus in life. Choose to think about all of the **positive** things you have going on in your life instead! Loving yourself and setting long-term goals as your main priorities are all that matter, especially when faced with insecurities. It doesn't hurt to have a friend or two to help you along the way with any problems you are dealing with and can offer you good advice. Most importantly (yes, I must repeat it), **remember always to love yourself first!**

Turbulence of Self-Esteem

Dajai Williams

"Young and Afraid"

Tosha R. Dearbone

As a young girl, I experienced something tragic. When I was 12 years old, I was molested by a man I held in high regard: my grandmother's boyfriend. Up until that day, I thought he was the greatest man ever and never saw any wrong in him.

On Memorial Day of 2013, I was in my room watching television when he came in and just stared at me. I **immediately** sensed something was wrong. His whole demeanor had changed in an instant, leaving me to feel as if I didn't even know the man who stood before me. Suddenly, he started to touch me in places I shouldn't have been touched. He also licked my feet and ears. I tried to kick him off of me, but because he's six-feet tall and weighed more than 200 pounds, I couldn't move him. When I started to scream, he finally stopped and left me lying there in the bed.

As soon as I could, I ran to the living room to try to wake up my grandmother, but she wouldn't budge. I then ran out of the house to my neighbor's and asked to call my mother. At first, I couldn't get through to her, so I called my sister and stepdad. When my sister pulled up, I noticed my cousin and aunt came in another car as well. My sister immediately jumped out of the car and went off on him. He tried to leave in my grandmother's truck because he knew my stepdad was on the way, but my family members blocked the driveway with their cars so that he couldn't go anywhere.

My grandmother must have been awakened by the ruckus going on outside because when she joined us, she called **me** a liar and said he *never* touched me! She was very mean to me and took his side.

Turbulence of Self-Esteem

So, when my stepdad arrived, the police were with him. My stepdad tried to beat down "granddad," but the police wouldn't let him through. My mom came just as the police were taking "granddad" away. As soon as she saw me, she ran over and hugged me.

The police said I needed to go to the hospital to get a rape kit done. While there, the staff checked the places where I had been licked. They, of course, found his saliva on my feet and ears. I then had to go to the police station to give a report that detailed all of what happened to me. I grew tired of having to repeat the same story over and over again to many different people. The police told my mom and me that they didn't want me to go to court because I would have to face "granddad" there, and they didn't want me to go through that experience at such a young age. After leaving the police station, I went to my cousins' house. My mom and sister returned to my grandmother's house to get my clothes.

After I was molested, I was **devastated** and fell into a deep, depressed swamp. I soon started to blame myself for what happened. All types of things were going through my head, such as:

- ❖ "*I should have* left the room when he came in."
- ❖ "*I should have* stayed at home and not at grandma's house."
- ❖ "*I should have* pretended to be asleep."

I didn't do any of those things because I was not expecting him to do anything to me.

A lot of time had passed with me beating myself up over the incident. My mom and dad always tried cheering me up.

They did everything they could think to do, but I still wasn't that happy, little girl everyone knew.

The change came for me when I joined a group called "Positive Express." Positive Express is a group for young girls who battle with low self-esteem and who have been through various tragedies in life. For some reason, I instantly clicked with the Mentor, Ms. Tosha. When I first met her, I was afraid to tell her about what happened to me. After a few group meetings, I became more comfortable being around her, so I told her my story. I was surprised at the reaction I received from her! She hugged me tightly and told me, *"You are a strong, young lady who needs to pray and ask for healing."* I will never forget those words.

I started praying to God, asking to be healed…but then I stopped—and fell into the swamp again. I cried myself to sleep every night, wouldn't eat, and punished myself for the decision made by a person who couldn't keep his hands to himself.

After attending a few events with Positive Express, there is one that stands out the most. At the event, there was a pretty lady there who shared her story of how she had been hurt. As she told her story, I listened attentively. She shared how she had been at a bar or nightclub when she was drugged and then taken advantage of. Someone actually spiked her drink and then did whatever they wanted to do with her. She explained that for a while, she felt she was the one to blame and that she hated herself and her life. Soon, she realized she was not to blame. Once she realized that, she knew she had to forgive the man who hurt her, so she surrounded herself with nothing but positivity.

Turbulence of Self-Esteem

From her story, I learned that even though "granddad" hurt me and tried to take advantage of me, I had to forgive him so that I could be happy and not filled with hatred toward him for the rest of my life. I knew I had worth. Although I had a lot of anger built up inside, I had to let it go to realize my worth and nothing less. To tell you the truth, it's the best thing I have ever done! I have been at peace with myself over that storm for a while now. I had the **best** support system from my family, especially my mom and sister. They never turned their backs on me when I was going through all of that.

I also began to write out my feelings and then just ball them up and throw them in the trash. That was my way of releasing the pain without having to talk to anyone about it anymore.

Then, I met my best friend. When I told her my story, she immediately grabbed and held me tightly. She helped me even more because no other outsiders knew about my problem. She encouraged me to open about the experience, as keeping it all in was very toxic. Once I started talking openly about my past experience, other females began to approach me and tell me about what they had been through. It felt good trying to help others who have also been through similar types of hurt, torment, and embarrassment.

I have since healed and become a better person than I was before. I have many people to thank, for they showed me that I am both loved *and* truly blessed.

The things that helped me the most were prayer and ambition. I had to take charge of my life and not keep feeling bad for myself. I had to "toughen up"! I still think about the time in my life when I felt I had no one—no family or friends in which to confide. I felt so alone. However, even when I was hurting, I played it cool. I had no other choice but to be strong-minded. I refused to allow "granddad" to defeat me ever again!

Ms. Tosha was the one who helped me realize my inner strength. She is the reason I can talk about what happened to me without shedding a tear. She taught me how to *effectively* cope with a lot of things that happen in my life. Honestly, being a part of Positive Express when I needed those services the most was really helpful. I am very grateful for being a part of something so magnificent!

If I'm honest, I wanted my life to be over with at one point. I didn't want to see anyone or anything. I was in a dark, isolated place where I felt I was ugly and filled with bad luck. For example, while I was in school, I told a few girls who I thought were friends about the molestation. They did exactly what I had hoped they wouldn't do; went around the school telling people about it and switching up my words. When my sophomore year of high school came around, a girl walked up to me and said, *"You're the girl who got raped. You probably deserved it."* I was so stunned, all I did was walk away and cry. I was shocked about how my words had been changed like that! Only three girls knew at the time, so it was disappointing to be betrayed by someone I considered to be a "friend."

Being a child—a little girl—is hard, but we are stronger than we give ourselves credit for. We are able to build ourselves up and handle things as best we can. That's what I had to do. The moral of my story, ladies, is this: **No one or nothing can tear you down but you.** You *have* to overcome it all. God wouldn't put you through "it" if He, for any reason whatsoever, thought you couldn't handle it!

Tosha R. Dearbone

Turbulence of Self-Esteem

Destiny Walker

"Overcoming Low Self-Esteem"

Tosha R. Dearbone

*"You are utterly beautiful, my dearest;
there is not a single flaw in you..."*
~ Song of Solomon 4:7 ~

What I love the most about that Bible verse is how God allows us to realize how beautiful our flaws are. I believe you must get uncomfortable in order to be fully comfortable. I know, I know; easier said than done, right? Let me explain my reasoning so that you can grasp this important message about how I overcame my low self-esteem.

Getting uncomfortable in order to be fully comfortable within yourself is no easy task. You must "free yourself" to do the things you do best and then compliment yourself for doing those things afterward. It's like doing your hair the way you want and then looking in the mirror and saying, **"WOW! LOOK AT WHAT I DID!"** I looked at myself in the mirror one day and felt truly beautiful because I had done something I wanted to do...just for me. I embraced the enchanting beauty that was already given to me.

Think about it like this: While you were being created, God didn't say, *"I'm going to design her just for her looks and nothing else."* Your looks should not define who you are; they should **complement** who you are in addition to those things you sometimes do that are outside of the box that both you **and** others place you into. Invest more time into you, no matter what. Treat yourself to something that makes you feel marvelous, such as getting your nails done or eyebrows waxed. Why is that important? Because treating yourself is reflective of loving yourself! Oh! And most importantly, don't allow those silly boys to define what you do or who you are.

Turbulence of Self-Esteem

I read one of Joel Osteen's books called *Think Better; Live Better* (yes, I like to read — and I know you like to read, too, because you're reading this book). Anyway, Joel's book helps the reader think and live better. So, where does it all begin? It starts in that beautiful mind of yours and what you believe can affect you — both positive and negative things. You have to get out of that low self-worth stage you may be in at this moment and start acknowledging your intelligence! In Joel's book, he said, *"You can easily go around feeling bad, having low self-esteem and self-worth, but never let what someone did keep you from knowing who you are."* I really felt that when I read it! What about you?

When God created you, He said, *"I've created **another** masterpiece!"* Sometimes, you have to look in at your heart and acknowledge the gifts God placed inside of you **before** you were formed in your mother's womb.

I remember feeling as if I wasn't beautiful enough or good enough for God to use. I had a nasty attitude, too. One day, I realized I couldn't listen to the judgment going on all around me. I did more of what made me happy, no matter what that looked like to everyone else. God spoke to my heart and told me, *"You look so beautiful when you're happy!"* I even spent time talking to myself in the mirror affirming that **I'm beautiful, I'm strong, I'm enough, I'm powerful, I'm confident,** and **I'm smart**. I believed what God said about me — and now, it's time for you to do the same.

Now, don't get me wrong: Being 100% honest and transparent here, I still struggle a *little* with low self-esteem. The difference, however, is that I put God first and know that I don't need attention from others to make me feel beautiful. All I needed was to give my attention to our Creator! When I told

Him about my insecurities, He turned them into my breakthroughs. I released those bad "labels" others put on me…and the ones I placed on myself:

- ❖ *"I'm not beautiful."*
- ❖ *"I'm not enough."*
- ❖ *"I'm not good enough."*
- ❖ *"My style isn't up-to-date."*

It's not healthy for your mind, body, or soul to keep those negative thoughts locked up inside. Don't you dare hold onto them for one more minute!

Be sure never to allow a boy to validate who you are. The chances are likely that if you were to share with him all of your insecurities (such as thinking you're not beautiful), that same boy might use that information against you. How, you wonder? He could easily manipulate and control you because you will find yourself dependent on him to make you feel better about yourself. Under no circumstance is that behavior okay. Making that boy your #1 priority is dangerous to your overall health and doesn't aid in building your self-esteem. Think about this: If he were to leave you, he might leave you feeling like an "easy catch" because all he wanted was something from you. Who will you cry to then? Who will be your center of attention in his absence?

Let me share a secret with you: **You must start placing positive labels on yourself so that you will eventually start believing them!** We speak life or death over our own lives. God's Word says to be careful of what we say because our tongue holds *power*.

Turbulence of Self-Esteem

Repeat after me:

"I am powerful!"

"I am enough!"

"I am well and able!"

"I will prosper!"

I am declaring today that you will overcome low self-esteem and self-worth. You will come to know and value your worth; it's just a matter of time.

I had to grow up to **"GLOW UP."** I had to humble myself, too. Many of us girls have low self-esteem because of absent fathers. Let me be the one to tell you that **GOD** is your Father! He designed you to be exactly who you are today. Even if you don't know about God, think about what I just told you. Out of *millions* of other girls your age, He chose **YOU**. He knows who you really are already, so it's up to you to receive what He says about you, such as:

- ❖ *"You're so beautiful."*
- ❖ *"You're priceless."*
- ❖ *"You're worth more than money and gold."*
- ❖ *"You're fortunate that the Fortune [the Holy Spirit] is within you."*

For example, if you were to view a diamond that's covered with dirt, it wouldn't be that appealing to you because it "looks cheap." Take that same diamond and clean it up back to shiny and new, and you will fall **so** in love with it!

In the same context, just because you may not look appealing to others doesn't mean you can't shine—especially after you wash off all of those bad labels. You're still alive! You have unsurmountable strength! You can still change your self-attitude!

At one time, I was just like that dirty diamond. I had to get comfortable and wash all of that mess off of me. How did I do it? Well, I got out of my comfort zone and started investing time in **ME** instead of seeking attention from boys. **Trust me: Boys come, and boys go.** I had to remind myself that I come first, my body is a temple, and God has bigger plans for my life. When my relationship with God grew, those good labels enveloped me like the finest full-length fur coat you could ever imagine!

My self-esteem grew leaps and bounds when I started living for me! I began doing physical things like going outside for walks and dancing to my favorite songs while alone. Those simple things helped to make me feel better about myself. I also started drinking more water instead of sugary drinks to provide my body with better nourishment. There's far more to life than just the way one looks. I focused on what makes me feel beautiful, and it helped to raise my standards on what others thought of me at the same time.

One of the definitions of beautiful is "extremely excellent." As such, being beautiful stands for the joy that lives deep within each and every single one of us—the beauty that **GOD** has placed inside.

Be free! Be kind to others! Help to uplift a relative or friend who's discouraged or at her lowest point in life. I

Turbulence of Self-Esteem

promise you this: Once you realize you can help another, it will help to boost your self-esteem. I'm a witness. I've been through it. I've "been there, done that." I had to learn that outward beauty is based on one's **opinion**.

Close your eyes and imagine for a moment a world where you cannot see but only hear. There would be no judgment about one's looks. There would be no choice but to go by our character. We wouldn't have any other option than to create our own beauty because looks simply wouldn't matter!

To you, I say: Be a dreamer, young lady! Set your standards high and dream beautifully — with **extreme excellence**!

Tosha R. Dearbone

Turbulence of Self-Esteem

Gracie Greene

"I Am Beauty"

Tosha R. Dearbone

When I was a little girl, people always told me how pretty I was. No matter where I went, they would compliment me by saying how beautiful my eyes and smile were or mention the amount of hair I had on my head (which was a **LOT**). I loved going out with my parents because I knew without a shadow of a doubt that the compliments would be rolling in.

When my 7th-grade year came, I started attending a new school. After being home-schooled for five years, I had high hopes for what was to come. I just knew I was in for a welcomed change...*or so I thought.*

Not long after the school year began, some of my peers called me "ugly"! They went on to say that I wasn't smart and didn't fit in anywhere. In hopes of proving them wrong, I did my best to fit in, but it was all to no avail. They relentlessly made fun of me because they knew I was different from them. I didn't learn like them because I was a slow learner with Attention Deficit Hyperactivity Disorder (known as ADHD). Having ADHD left me feeling sad, alone, and in a bad mood all the time. I thought I was "dumb" and any other negative adjective you could name about my lack of intelligence.

Things only became more complicated for me when we moved into a first-floor apartment in Meyerland, Texas, two years later. The apartment looked nice but had a horrible smell that came from the nearby bayou. I honestly liked our new home at first, but then came to hate living there. I tried not to let my disdain show because I knew my parents were struggling. That didn't last long, however. When I could no longer hide my feelings, my attitude quickly changed. I openly expressed my hatred for having to move in the first place. I

Turbulence of Self-Esteem

moped around all day and wouldn't speak to anyone in my family. During this time, I also gained a lot of weight and lost the few friends I had. I didn't get out much (if at all) and stopped being my old, happy self. Suicidal thoughts actually invaded my mind.

Things only got worse for me when I had to give up the dog that I had since she was a puppy. For us to stay in our new apartment, we had to let her go. It hurt me so bad when she left. I cried so hard and shortly after that, things spiraled out of control for me. Although I tried not to be angry, it didn't work out that well. I loved my dog! She was like a child to me!

The destruction in my young life didn't stop there, though! Things grew progressively worse before getting better.

A few months into our living in the apartment, we learned the bayou was going to flood. Our family didn't know what to do or where to go. Fortunately, our upstairs neighbor, Andy, opened up his home to us. He told my dad we could stay in his apartment for the night. I felt relieved and was grateful for Andy's kind gesture. He saved us! Later that night, when Andy and my dad went to check on the damage to our downstairs apartment, five feet of water had swallowed up and destroyed everything in its path. That was a truly traumatic moment for me and had me thinking, **"What if Andy hadn't saved us? We could have been trapped in there!"** I realized it was no one but God who helped us by using our neighbor to keep us safe. I thanked God for His protection and a little later, fell back asleep. When I woke up the next morning to another cloudy August day in Andy's house, the power was out. I pulled the patio blinds to the side so that some light could break through the darkness and that's when I saw it:

Tosha R. Dearbone

The bayou was filled with so much water, it almost reached the second floor where we were staying!

What was truly traumatizing about this experience was that I had to ride all alone in an airlift operated by a helicopter directly above the floodwaters. Although nothing happened to me, the experience still haunts me to this day. I still get flashbacks from that moment.

The following day, we stayed at the George R. Brown Convention Center in downtown Houston, Texas, along with others who needed shelter from the floods. I vividly recall it being freezing cold inside with people filling up virtually every available space. I didn't like being around so many people. That night, we slept next to strangers, including a woman who snored loudly and then farted in her sleep. I will never forget her and pray I never have to endure another flood a day in my life!

We stayed there long enough for my mom to call my grandparents who had seen the whole story about the flood on the news. After my mom assured them we were safe and wanted to get out of the convention center, my grandparents arranged a ride for us, and we went to stay with them for a while. I had fun while staying with them. I'm grateful for their help. While there, I talked to my grandma about things that were bothering me. Just talking to someone made me feel better. I was also able to bond with my aunt while there.

Once things improved in the area, our family moved to a home in Sienna Plantation, Texas. I was still sad often but found that I had some happy moments as well. After we settled in, I was able to hang out with my best friend. I told her about

Turbulence of Self-Esteem

everything that happened when we went to the mall one day. That's when she told me she was dating. I was so happy for her but also sad because, for the first time, I wanted a boyfriend, too. It was then that I started to like boys. At the time, I was 16 years old and had never dated.

I remember going to my friend's birthday party that year. There was a guy there who I liked, but he didn't seem to even notice me. I brushed it off because there were plenty of other guys out there who I noticed. Unfortunately for me, they didn't pay me any attention either. I just stopped trying. I looked in the mirror often and thought about how ugly I must have seemed to those boys. Eventually, I hated looking in the mirror altogether. Things had gotten so bad for me and my self-esteem, I even considered plastic surgery. I started to hate having my picture taken or even looking at myself in photos. I also struggled with making and keeping new friends. When I would make one, it seemed as if they would suddenly disappear and no longer reply to my calls or texts. With all of this rejection going on in my life, I became antisocial and grew a genuine dislike for everyone and everything. My temper became short, and when I was mad, I used to slam and break things.

One day, I decided to reinvent myself. I told my mom I wanted to start wearing makeup, so she bought me some. Then, I decided I wanted to dress differently, so I started dressing like I cared more about myself. I shared with my mom I wanted a different hairstyle—straight instead of curly. When she straightened my hair, it didn't take it long to turn into a puffy mess. As such, I kept my hair in a bun most of the time. It was then I took notice that some boys started to pay me attention. A few months later, I started dressing more my age and wearing lip gloss and eyeshadow. Boys really started looking at me then! Around that same time, my passion for music came into play. I used to write rap songs about my feelings (music got me out of the funk I was in), prompting me to change my look once more.

Everywhere I went, people were looking at me again and giving me compliments. I felt my self-esteem begin to rise. I started walking with my shoulders up, and head held high with confidence. Slowly, I started taking pictures of myself and posting them on Instagram.

After all of that, I **still** didn't have a boyfriend. Inside, I felt awful about myself, but that didn't stop me from continuing to search for the attention I craved. It didn't even have to be a guy, just as long as I received a compliment from *someone*. I do believe some people did take notice but chose not to toss a compliment my way. Instead, they would look right past me as if they didn't see me. I slowly stopped going out and chose to stay inside when my parents went out.

Watching couples on TV shows or seeing pictures of happy couples added even more sadness to my life. I thought to myself, *"I wish I had that type of romance in my life."* I then became obsessed with the **idea** of love and romance. I would read romance books and then beat myself up over the fact that I didn't have a boyfriend. I became so desperate to date someone and longed to be asked out on a date. I constantly looked at my flaws, finding fault with so much about **ME**—leaving me to understand why no one wanted to date or get to know me. I became my own enemy by making fun of myself. I then started emotional eating again, causing me to gain a lot of weight.

Things started to change for me when my mom signed me up to volunteer at New Hope Church. I didn't go there expecting to meet anyone I would click with, but I did meet some good people nonetheless. Going to church helped me build my social status. I went there every Saturday and started attending their trainings. Later on, my mom signed me up for teen study night. On the first night, I was both excited and nervous. I didn't think I would meet anyone who'd like me, but I met five people who I meshed with right away. For the first time in a long time, I was truly happy! We exchanged telephone numbers and have been talking ever since.

Ever since that first Tuesday night, I have been feeling fabulous about myself. I not only talk to my friends about what's going on with me; I also talk to Miss Tosha. She helps me a lot when I go to her events and talk about my life with her. I feel so much better after releasing those things I've kept bottled up for so long. Not only do I talk about them; I also write and dance those negative thoughts away. Putting those words to song always helps me feel better. I cannot thank Miss Tosha and the other girls in the group enough for their support. I want to extend a special thank you to Miss Tosha because she is the one who helped me be a part of this book project after learning how much I like to write.

I recall the days when I would wake up with my mind focused on pleasing everyone else. I rarely spoke words that would boost my confidence. Now, I'm not as focused on what other people think about me. That's not to say that they don't get under my skin from time to time, but for the most part, I try not to let what they say or think get to me. I want to be a better 'ME' and not be so negative all the time. At one point, I allowed negative thoughts to cause me to stop enjoying life. I have since replaced those thoughts with positive ones, and better things are starting to happen in my life because of it!

I encourage you to stay positive and focused on the good things in your life. Trust me: It helps! Whatever you do, **don't give up!**

Turbulence of Self-Esteem

Havilyn "Greatest 1" Dawson

"My Testimony"
9/28/2017 – 10/3/2017

Tosha R. Dearbone

Lost of words of the death I felt within.
Felt like I was losing myself trying to fit in.
Not a crowd of people that reject the acceptance of a society that's insecure,
But trying to fit into a life that wasn't me.
Draining myself from a misconception of being perfect,
Thinking maybe my father would want me.
Maybe I won't be a disappointment and a statistic of a stereotypically black culture.
Black is just my skin, but my mental is a motion.
A motion of thoughts that are all clustered and trying to malfunction.
Consistent thoughts of perfection are swelling up in my brain.
It's really hard trying to be sane. Are we really normal?
Or is normal just what we say?
Normalizing my thoughts; how is that possible?
Thinking in the dark makes me have suicidal options.
Lying on the floor with tears down my face,
Thinking who I was going to disappoint today put me in a situation where I almost wasn't here today.
If it wasn't for God, that was my biggest mistake.
I should have prayed before I took a blade to slice my arm.
Almost deep, but not too deep;
Just how I feel for you, but I can't feel you.
Life took me on a rollercoaster.
I gave my whole life to you when you saved me.
I'm grateful. I could have been dead, but that blade helped me.
Helped me to realize I needed help.
God saved me.
Hit rock bottom, all I could do was rise.
I thrived, and all I could do was smile.
That's pride.

~ GREATEST 1 ~

Turbulence of Self-Esteem

"Bitter to Better"

Insecurity is the lack of confidence in yourself, uncertainty, or anxiety. Most people have insecurities because of past mistakes, broken relationships, and words spoken against them. I, myself, have dealt with insecurities with my appearance, from what I have done in my past, and the words people spoke against me. I doubted myself because of what I have done. My past could not be changed. It made me angry and bitter. I was unhappy with myself; so unhappy that I began to question myself and seek validation from people who were meaningless to me. My insecurities became a burden. They transformed me into a person people expected me to be when my true "self" was crying out. I began to harm myself because I felt as if I deserved the pain I caused myself for years. No one noticed I was unhappy. It took that last time when I wanted to take my life to be noticed.

I began to feed off the pain and regret from those insecurities. They were my best friends, and I blamed everything on my past and others—but I remained unhappy. I had to learn that I cannot be what my family and friends expect me to be. I can only be who I am. I am human, and I make mistakes, but as long as I learn from those mishaps, I see myself grow into the woman I intend to be.

Materialistic things and money will not help your insecurities. It's a cover-up to hide behind those things. Nothing is wrong with getting your nails and hair done. It's exciting and makes you feel good. After all, I, too, love to treat myself! But are you truly happy with yourself as a whole? Are you truly happy with the person you are? Are you still seeking validation from others? Are you the person you want to be?

Tosha R. Dearbone

    I asked myself those questions to make myself realize I have scars behind my insecurities. I needed to be healed so that I could become a better woman, not a bitter woman. Our insecurities end friendships and relationships because with insecurities comes a lack of trust, jealousy, envy…and the list goes on. I understand you have been rejected. I understand your heart is broken. I understand. But do not let what has affected you change you into someone you do not want to be. Take all the pain you've endured and let it go. Do daily affirmations, all while believing you are not what people say you are. Have confidence in yourself and be you. You're not perfect, but you are worth it. You are worth fighting for. You are beautifully and wonderfully made by the Man above. You just have to believe that.

    I learned how to trust in God and not in man. I had to believe that God created me to be different. It's okay to stand out. Why be like anyone else? Why should I settle for less? Take a moment to read Song of Solomon 4:7 in the Bible. Love is unconditional. It's worth seeking in God.

    I used to let people move my faith in myself. I thought I was not worthy of God blessing me. I believed I was not worthy of God's love, mercy, and grace. My self-esteem became so low, I started to look for love in the wrong places. I started to get attached to people, which made it hard for me to let them go when their season in my life was over. It also made it hard for me to love unconditionally because I had a corrupted mindset of me being against the world. I let my fear and other people control my emotions and how I felt about myself.

    I learned how to remove the toxic people from my life. I had to get healed and check myself from time to time because sometimes, there's something in us that attracts certain types of people. The more we attract those people, the more we damage ourselves because we tend to try to "fix" people and be what they expect us to be. In reality, we cannot help ourselves because we aren't healed. We hold onto our past, creating deep scars. Those scars develop into insecurities. For years, my dad and I haven't seen eye-to-eye. I had so much built up anger and was bitter for a long time. Every time I thought I forgave him, I really hadn't. I held onto that baggage and dragged it into relationships with other people. It made it hard to trust people and in myself because I felt like I wasn't wanted and wasn't worth keeping. I treated myself accordingly and, every time, I expected to be hurt—until I changed my mindset and let go of the pain. Slowly, the insecurities started to fade, and my scars started to heal.

~~~~~~~~~~~~~

THREE GOLDEN RULES I ESTABLISHED FOR MYSELF

#1: DON'T LET THE BLIND LEAD YOU.

Just like a leach, he's just going to drain you.

The blind is a sinner, but you're just another sinner.

While he's eating his cake, you're wondering why you are cold in the winter.

How can he lead you when he cannot see you?

Your destiny is greater than a mustard seed.

I just need you to believe it.

#2: DON'T LET ANYONE DECEIVE YOU.

They talk behind your back, and then they leave you

To pick up the pieces you never dropped, but if we were focused

On the mission, we would have never stopped.

People can be toxic, and people can have great intentions,

But if it's not from God, pay them no attention.

#3: DON'T BE SIMPLE-MINDED…

Because greatness is within you.

Never stay in the box because God won't mislead you.

God is waiting; He would never forsake you. Believe in God,

You will believe in yourself. All things through Him are possible,

So, it's no doubting about who's next.

Turbulence of Self-Esteem

MESSAGE TO ALL QUEENS

You are beautiful,
Despite what anybody thinks.
God created you.
That's a wonderful thing!
He made no mistakes.

Don't listen to what they say.
Your black is beautiful.
Don't ever confuse that with the hate.
Don't let males define you.
Queens, does he seek value?

Embrace your natural,
Embrace the insecurities.
You are beautiful.
Know your worth,
Know yourself, and be you.

Be with someone who loves you for you;
Not for your curves
Or for the cake.
Something that's so sacred,
Let it be worth more to you.

Respect yourself and make him respect you.
Don't degrade yourself
By letting society call you out of your name.
Queen, that's not you.

Tosha R. Dearbone

Queens, by walking into this season,
You need to embrace yourself.
I need you to know,
God said that your worth is more than rubies.
Believe that.

Self-love starts with you.
Receive that.
Queens, you are…
You are beautiful.
I mean that.

Queens, you don't have to
Show your breasts to get his attention.
You don't need a bigger booty
To be like the celebrities in the pictures.
You don't need to be like
The girls in the movies
Who take shots and lifts
To make their face look stiffer,
Lips look fuller,
Waist look tighter.

They degrade themselves for cash
That doesn't even last longer than the surgery.
Queens, don't be deceived by what you see.
They have problems just like you and me.
Why do you think they find something wrong?

Turbulence of Self-Esteem

Trying to hide the stitches,
But we know what's going on.
Life is not perfect, and we are just human,
But God made no mistake making Queens.
We have to become a union.

You are Black.
You are White.
You are Asian.
You are Latino.
You are you, and that is beautiful.

Queens, you are beautiful!
You are the light!
You are worth more than a million stars!
We love you just the way you are.
Smile. That is all you have to do.

But most importantly,
Just Be YOU.

~ GREATEST 1 ~

Tosha R. Dearbone

Turbulence of Self-Esteem

Jadah Jones

"What I Didn't Know About Me"

Tosha R. Dearbone

"It is not the mountain we conquer, but ourselves."
~ **Sir Edmund Hillary** ~

Every day, I am learning more about who I am. It has been challenging at times. There are periods in my life when I don't feel like the prettiest, smartest, or smallest. No matter how many compliments I receive, all of my thoughts lead back to this one question:

"Am I truly wonderfully and fearfully made by God or was I just a creation that He was experimenting with and forgot to come back to?"

Well, through this "learning" process, I have discovered that I am, indeed, wonderfully and fearfully made! I have also learned things about myself that I didn't even know. I hope that by sharing what I've learned about me, it will help a young lady realize she is exactly who God created her to be!

My story…

At the age of 13, my body began to fill out fast. I had a big butt and big boobs—as well as people assuming I was having sex and being grown. In my case, I come from a family of full-figured women. God gave me some extra. *(Jadah rolls her eyes and sighs.)* I'm not sure if it's a curse or a blessing, but I do know with surety that I've had mixed emotions about my appearance as far back as I can remember.

I have heard people talk about me and voice their opinions—ones that have really hurt my feelings. That negative talk changed my whole demeanor of how I thought about myself and my body. Because I had a little extra weight on me, I was called "fat." There were even rumors spread about me

Turbulence of Self-Esteem

that said I was pregnant! I fell into a depression and tried to do things to make me lose weight (I'm sure some of those things were unhealthy, but at the time, I didn't care). I wanted people to stop talking about me and making me feel as if I was the scum under their shoes. Perhaps you can imagine the countless sleepless nights I had while searching for a quick fix. I truly thought something was wrong with me! I embraced the lies that people whispered about me:

- *Fat.*
- *Ugly.*
- *Useless.*
- *I had no place…anywhere.*

I'm unsure how my mom knew I was battling self-esteem issues, but one day, she came to me, and we had a conversation about the true meaning of being "beautiful." She asked me, *"What do you think the true meaning of beautiful is?"*

"I don't know, mom."

Now, I know that sounds sad, but it was my truth. I had no clue what real beauty was because I had allowed my peers and the media to paint that picture. Well, because I had no idea what true beauty was, my mom gave me a small assignment — one I encourage you to do as well.

First, she gave me the following scripture:

"Your beauty should come from outward adornments, such as elaborate hairstyles and the wearing of gold jewelry or fine clothes. Rather, it should be that of your inner self, the unfading beauty of a gentle and quiet spirit, which is of great worth in God's sight."
~ **1 Peter 3:3-4** ~

She then gave me a stack of sticky notes and had me write down a bunch of different affirmations that I stuck to my mirror. My mom instructed me to read them first thing in the morning and before I went to bed each night.

TRUTH: What you speak about yourself either makes or breaks you.

Following is the list of affirmations my mother had me write on my sticky notes. I encourage you to write them down or make your own. Place them where you can see and read them aloud daily.

I am who God says I am.	I am smart.
I am blessed.	I am a leader.
I am enough.	I am confident.
I am limitless.	I am grateful.
I am successful.	I am beautiful inside and out.
I am courageous	I am a scholarship recipient.
I am a great listener.	I am able to do anything.
I am loved.	I am strong and healthy.
I am a trendsetter.	I am disciplined.
I am honest and trustworthy.	I am a believer in my dreams.
I am kind to others, and they are kind to me.	I am of great worth.
I am in love with myself.	I am wise and determined.
I am capable of thinking for myself.	I am not perfect.
I am passionate and talented.	I am true to my heart.
I am IT.	I am the joy the world is waiting for.

Turbulence of Self-Esteem

The more I spoke those words, something connected them to my heart. I am **MORE** than what people know. The things that people said about me began to phase me no longer. The more I sat with my mom and just talked about how I felt about myself, I realized there were bad seeds I planted within myself that grew and ruined the true understanding of how **GOD** felt about me.

There are a lot of girls who would never admit what I'm about to share with you; however, it's my truth. I want to help you understand that no matter what mistakes you've made, you are not your mistakes.

I am guilty of looking for love in the wrong places. Indeed, I had "daddy issues." I felt that liking boys and doing what they wanted me to do would win me a "forever spot" with them. Wrong, Sis! The worst thing I could have done was have sex with a guy, thinking he really wanted to be with me. Having sex before marriage was a part of my low self-esteem blow. I thought, *"He's going to call me. He cares about me. He loves me!"* **Sis, please!** I made that mistake a couple of times before I learned that boys are out here to place my name on their list and boost up their ego.

My mom shared with me that when a guy cares about me, he will wait for me. She also explained what God's grace is and helped me to start over. No, I am not a virgin. So, how can I start over? Well, I am on a purity journey to abstain from having sex again until I am married.

Will there be fine guys galore? Yes!

Will I be tempted? Yes!

Has God given me a way out of all that madness? **Absolutely!**

Never let anyone tell you that you can't start over and make it right with you and God because I did!

I have searched for love from my family and, at times, it wasn't there to be found. People who are supposed to be there to love me haven't been. I have looked at my friend's family and thought, *"They have the world's best family!"* I have been searching for love for a while. The absence of my biological father has taken its toll on me. Trying to be comfortable in my own skin has taken a toll on me as well. Each of these different things has affected my self-esteem to the point I have sometimes felt invisible, numb, and even questioned my existence on this Earth.

There is a book that my mentor co-authored called *Walk With Her: Wisdom for Her Teenage Journey*. A woman named Ms. Stephanie wrote one chapter in the book. In her chapter, there was a part that caught my eye. Ms. Stephanie said, ***"You're not only beautiful; you're also a valuable young lady."*** I read that statement repeatedly. I now carry that statement in my spirit daily because it's past time that I see myself the way **GOD** sees me! (Up until that moment, I hadn't paid much attention to my value. I began to treat myself like a diamond, locked away in a case so that not just anyone could touch me. One must have an eye for expensive things to even *see* me — let alone *touch* me.)

Turbulence of Self-Esteem

In closing, I leave you with the things I have learned about myself along the way to rebuilding my self-esteem:

- ❖ I really am loved! (I was loved all along.)
- ❖ I am still searching for my purpose in life. I know I have one, though! (You have a purpose, too.)
- ❖ I know my value! Can you say, *"I am expensive, Honey"*? #KingdomKid
- ❖ I never have to do anything out of character to please a boy or anyone else.
- ❖ I genuinely want to see my sisters heal and win! #MySistersKeeper
- ❖ I am not my mistakes!

Self-esteem is a matter of growth and maturity that we need to take the time to deal with. In time, we will heal. Realize that we are often too hard on ourselves. The more we feed those negative lies in our heads, they will surely grow. **BUT** when we begin to uproot those lies and plant positive things in their place, only then will we be the beautiful bouquet of roses that God sees.

I love you, Girl! It's time to glow up!

Love,

Jadah

Tosha R. Dearbone

Turbulence of Self-Esteem

Je'Nora Lynn

"H.E.R. – His Eminent Reflection"

Tosha R. Dearbone

Let me begin my story by taking a trip down memory lane...

H.E.R. is *ME* — a little girl born on December 19, 1988, in Houston, Texas, who was hit with many challenges while growing up. Nevertheless, I'm still standing!

I was raised in a single-parent home with an older brother. My mom, brother, and I lived with our grandmother (my mother and father never married). At an early age, the insecurities I had about myself started to be a reflection I would face for many years to come. My images as a valued little girl were never secured by my father. I didn't know what it felt like to be "Daddy's Little Girl" until later in life. The impression I had of what a young girl/woman was came from the strength I saw in my grandmother (without the aid of my grandfather). I saw a woman who worked hard and raised her children — before aiding in raising her grandchildren (my brother and me).

My mother worked and did what she knew how to do, but I received a lot of backlash in the form of harsh words from the adults in the family. The words sounded like this:

- ❖ *"You're going to be just like your mother."*
- ❖ *"You're not going to finish things you started because she didn't either."*
- ❖ *"You're going to keep going from here to there."*

Each word was a deliberate blow to my self-esteem. I have no doubt many of you can relate to those statements in one way or another.

Although I enjoyed spending time outdoors, I valued my sleep and loved my dolls, doing hair, and taking care of my

Turbulence of Self-Esteem

younger **and** older cousins. At the young age of eight, I found great joy in doing hair, as it was an escape from the pain, rejection, hurt, low self-esteem, and feelings of defeat I endured…along with fear of a molester who was an older cousin I looked up to like an uncle.

I felt as though I couldn't say anything because I believed no one would listen. Being sheltered by my family never discussing issues related to molestation left me feeling all alone. I was also advanced mentally in the way my granny groomed me to look out for my family. She taught me that nothing or no one came before family. That stuck with me like a mouse on a mouse trap. I didn't want **any** shame to fall on anyone in our family, especially when I was told I was "like a daughter" to him.

Remember I said that my dad wasn't around a lot during my childhood? Well, as a result, I had a false image of what a father/daughter relationship was, except for what I had seen with my uncles and cousins. I was often left to feel like the "Black Sheep" of the family because my cousins had relationships with their fathers, coupled with the fact that I had a darker skin tone than some of them. I would try to fit in, not knowing until later in life that I wasn't *designed* to fit in. Even in middle school when Keds, Melissa's, denim skirts, and the doughnut hairstyle were trending, I tried unsuccessfully to fit in and figure out who I was.

At the time, my mom wasn't very active in my life, so I stayed at my granny's home—sheltered, forgotten about, and abandoned. I was a little girl who felt like she had no parent outside of my grandmother. I recall when my menstrual cycle started, it was my *great-aunt* who taught me what a pad was.

The mother/daughter bond many of my friends had was virtually nonexistent in my life. When my brother and I spent time with our mom, it was at her fiancé's house (which was his mother's house) or hanging out with them and then heading right back home to my grandmother's house. I was okay with that "arrangement," but it came at a cost: **My self-image became me believing I needed a man to validate me and that he came first.**

I remember fighting for my mom's love and attention. I would do things such as fail in school, just so she would come and fuss at me. Yes, it was negative attention, but at least she was paying attention to me, right? There were times she would get my brother while I was asleep to spend one-on-one time with him. When I would wake up and ask where my brother was, my granny would tell me, *"He left with your mom."* When my brother returned, I would ask why he didn't wake me, and his response would hurt me to the core:

"Mom told me not to."

The battle with my self-image raged on. Then, pile on top of it that there was a betrayer in my own home! I began to feel as if my mother despised me but loved my brother more.

Let's fast-forward to my mom moving back home during my 9th-grade year. I was excited at first because I just **knew** we were finally going to be a family again for real this time. Nope. I was wrong.

At the age of 14, my life made a major shift when I was molested by **another** man who was very dear to me. I was being touched on and didn't really understand all that was wrong with it because molestation was not a topic discussed in my home. As well, the same thing happened to me when I was younger, with the only differences this time being my age and who it was. I remember crying out to God saying, *"Please don't let me die here! I promise to help other girls and boys know that they can come out from this!"* I also recall suicide attempts because I was suffering in silence while hiding the pain behind a pretty smile and makeup. The man told me he would hurt my family if I said anything because he refused to go to jail and do time. How could I tell anyone? I would have put my family in harm's way! I was, after all, the protector of others. As long as he touched me and no one else, I was okay with the abuse.

In August 2005, I entered my senior year of high school. I decided to open up about the molestation and told my best friend. She held my hand every step of the way, starting with me telling my school counselor. I then went through Child Protective Services (CPS) assigned therapy, Houston Police Department (HPD) investigations, a lie detector test, and was permanently placed in the care of my grandmother (because of my age, I wasn't put in foster care, which is typical in these types of cases).

I graduated from high school in May 2006, thinking I was going to be okay and live a normal life. **NOPE!** My violator served *NO TIME!* Even though I passed the lie detector test, I was not believed. All the while, something in me kept saying, *"I went through this for a reason."*

On November 30, 2008, I gave birth to a son. I was very proud of myself because despite the odds being stacked against me, I was in college working towards getting my Cosmetology License and Associate's degree. During that time, I was in a relationship with someone I thought would be my "forever love." I thought he could do no wrong and placed him and his needs above my own—just as I had been shown for many years. Unfortunately, domestic violence was a facet of the relationship that came as a result of me catching him in lies about dealing with other women. Still, I remained with him for 9 ½ years, thinking he was all that I deserved. We would break up and get back together often during that time and, when we weren't together, I was a promiscuous woman.

That promiscuity led me into a homosexual relationship that lasted 3 ½ years. I had become bitter and wanted nothing to do with men due to my twisted viewpoint on the male persuasion dating back to my youth. Even though I had beaten the odds as a single mother with a license in Cosmetology obtained in 2009, my self-image was still jaded.

Around the beginning of 2012, my soul-searching journey began after trying everything else and failing. That's when I decided to give **GOD** a try—and *THAT'S* when everything changed for the better! I moved into my own place, bought my own car, held down **two** jobs, and was a college student—all while raising my son on my own. I learned I had to redefine who I was through the eyes of Christ. Once I began laying it all out on the table and at His feet, I picked up the image of Christ. The process wasn't easy, but it was definitely worth it! The most important thing I did was **FORGAVE MYSELF AND ALL OF MY ABUSERS.** I began *embracing* makeup instead of hiding behind it.

In April 2013, I met the man who would become my husband. We married in August 2013. I put him through so much early on and made life difficult for him. Even though I knew who I was in Christ, I still had a negative image of men

Turbulence of Self-Esteem

that I had to overcome. For some time, my husband couldn't touch me at all. My very *soul* had been molested, not just my body. I needed a **spiritual detox**. I had to be real about my feelings and what happened to me to even begin trusting my husband fully. That detox afforded me the opportunity to see all of the **GOOD** in my **BAD** "situations."

"Restore Me Makeup" was birthed in December 2017. I use makeup as an essential tool to aid broken, bruised, and low self-esteem women (like I once was) to take the journey to heal from the inside out so that they, too, can become **H.E.R.: His Eminent Reflection.** The restored **ME** is now a Prophetess of the Most High God, His essential mouthpiece to snatch back the identity of His bridegroom.

It took going back to the root of my issue and true forgiveness for both of my violators (as well as myself) to get to this new place in Christ. I had to get on my face before God and allow Him to restore me, clean me up, and make me new. Today, my makeup is now a light that shines so all may see my good works, and glorify my Father which is in Heaven!

I pray my story helps you become restored in your rebirth of **H.E.R.!**

Tosha R. Dearbone

Turbulence of Self-Esteem

Jiherra Daniels

"I'm Not Alone"

Tosha R. Dearbone

Being a victim of sexual assault can cause many negative triggers to arise. Horrible flashbacks, frustration, and bouts of confusion are very common responses to **any** form of victimization. If you believe you are being assaulted or even harassed in some type of way, don't allow it to continue because you are powerful and beautiful in *EVERY* kind of way. Above all else, know you're not alone. Others have endured **and** survived being victimized — including me.

Following is my story...

I was an average 11-year-old. I had a few people I called "friends," but pretty much stayed to myself most of the time. I never thought someone would try to hurt and humiliate me, until that one dreadful Wednesday afternoon at school...

I recall being excited because it was the middle of the week. What I thought would turn out to be a perfect day wasn't. It seemed like everything came crashing down on me at once rather unexpectedly. I was in 5th-period class when the assault happened.

Our regular teacher wasn't there that day, so we had a substitute. When my two friends and I finished our work, we approached the substitute and asked if we could get on the computer, which she allowed. At the time, there was only one computer available out of the three in the class, so my friends and I decided to take turns. As well, there was only one chair available at the computer station. One of my friends used a walker, so she did not need the seat. The other friend and I took turns sitting in the chair while the other used the computer. After I was done playing my game, I stood up to allow my friend to have a seat to play hers.

Turbulence of Self-Esteem

After I had been standing for a while, my back started to hurt. I bent over to stretch and ease the tension on my back. Suddenly, everyone in the class burst out laughing, but I didn't let it bother me...*at first.* When I found out the laughter was because this boy, whom I barely knew, rubbed his private part against me as I bent over, confusion set in. I didn't know how to react. I was filled with so many mixed emotions. A load of questions flashed through my mind:

- *"DID THAT JUST HAPPEN?"*
- *"OH, MY GOD! IS THIS A DREAM?"*
- *"IS THIS REAL?"*
- *"WHY, GOD? WHY?"*

I just **knew** I was going to lose it! I didn't deserve for that to happen to me. I was scared, upset, and didn't know what to do. That boy was a stranger to me, so it's not like I asked for his offensive attention. *Why did he do that to me?* I felt **horrible**. I kept asking myself over and over again, *"Why did you let him do that to you?"*

The following day, I was scared to go to the classes that I had with him because I felt very uncomfortable and lonely. It was as if someone had stuffed me in a tiny box in a dark room and left me there.

Eventually, I used my voice and found the strength to tell one of my closest friends about the incident. She explained to me that it was **not** my fault and reassured me that I was *strong* and *beautiful*. She also promised that she would be by my side every step of the way. We decided to approach one of our teachers after class. During that class, I wanted to burst out in tears, but I held them back. When class was over, I didn't want to stay at first. I'm grateful for my friend, though. She convinced me to stay so that I could finally get it off of my chest.

I explained to the teacher everything that happened the day before, and she said, *"No one — mark my words —* **NO ONE** *is supposed to touch you in a way you do not like.* **PERIOD!**" She then escorted my friend and me to the principal's office where we shared with her the same story. The principal's body language and attitude made it appear as if she didn't care about me being violated one bit — which hurt me even more. The principal then said in an accusatory tone, "*So, you went a whole day without telling me what happened? I don't believe it.*"

I sat there in shock for a moment, then stood up and walked out of her office. I then went to see the school counselor. After waiting for about five minutes, the counselor called me in, and I again explained everything that happened, including my time with the principal **and** her response. She told me she was going to follow up with the principal, but she never did.

A couple of days later, I finally decided to open up to my mom and tell her about the incident. My mom seemed both angry **and** shocked at the same time. Mom and I had a long talk, and she promised justice for me. The next day, my mom called the principal. She was *furious* because **not one adult** had contacted her and told her what happened to me…and a week had gone by! My principle caught a good tongue-lashing from my mom because of what she said to me — basically calling me a liar.

A couple more days go by, and my mom and mentor, Ms. Tosha, went to my school. They had a discussion with the principal and asked why **nothing** was done when I told her

Turbulence of Self-Esteem

about the incident. They also wanted to know why a serious situation such as sexual assault was taken so lightly. When my mom and Ms. Tosha were there, I was kind of scared but also relieved at the same time because something was **finally** being done.

Someone heard me! Someone listened and took action on my behalf!

Even after the adult intervention, I was still sad, upset, and embarrassed for quite some time. I couldn't shake the thought that it was all my fault because I *"let it happen."*

Things changed for me when I entered a program called "Child Advocates." My therapist helps me work through all of my problems, provides comfort, and makes me feel better through my worst of times.

Even though my situation was tragic, I have since grown both mentally and physically. I used to let itty-bitty things get under my skin and knock me down, but not anymore! I truly believe I am **STRONG** and **BEAUTIFUL**! I have learned to fight back mentally **AND** *(should the need arise)* physically!

Tosha R. Dearbone

Turbulence of Self-Esteem

Kristian Bell

"There is Beauty in My Teeth"

Tosha R. Dearbone

My battle with self-esteem started when I was in intermediate school. People would always ask me, *"What's wrong with your teeth?"* You see, although all of my baby teeth fell out and my adult teeth grew in their place, it still looks as if I have baby teeth—except for the two front ones. I guess since my teeth never really developed properly, people insisted on making fun of the way they looked.

I was only a little girl, so I didn't put too much thought into their teasing. I figured I would get braces by the time middle school came, and I wouldn't have to worry about it anymore. The first few months of middle school were a breeze! Nobody made fun of me or called me out about my teeth "situation." Then, I had to relocate to a new city, which placed me in a new and different school. Almost everywhere I looked, there were pretty girls; those who needed their teeth straightened wore braces, and all the **others** who had been made fun of for their appearance in years prior were growing into their looks. Although in stark comparison to "everyone else," I didn't allow things to affect me too much. I thought to myself, *"Well, maybe I'll be at their level before I start high school."* The rest of my middle school days flew by relatively smooth. People were very kind to me. I can't recall a time when someone pointed out my teeth during my 7th- and 8th-grade years, so I found myself smiling a lot more often.

Then, my 9th-grade year came...

High school can be brutal! People bluntly point out others' flaws and not think twice about how the "flawed" people felt about it. Teenagers can be very judgmental about any and everything, especially if you're *different* from them. It's like if you don't have certain traits that are **perfect**, you're automatically labeled a "lame" person. That judgment has nothing to do with one's personality, but rather solely on how a person looked on the outside. That alone was the determining factor as to whether or not someone would be accepted by the "in-crowd."

My peers made fun of me for my teeth, how skinny I was, my flat chest (and how the combination of those things made me ugly), and the shoes I would wear (they claimed my shoes were "old" and that I must have been too broke to get newer ones). The taunting went on for a few months, leading me to begin believing the things they said about me. Half of me felt like what they said wasn't true, but the **OTHER** half embraced what they said as truth because a lot of people kept saying the same things about me.

As a result, my self-esteem lowered tremendously to the point where I **never** smiled. I would wear padded bras, layer my clothes so that I wouldn't look so skinny, and even ate peanut butter straight from the jar so that I could gain more weight. Rarely would I smile and, when I did, it was because I laughed—but then I'd *quickly* cover my mouth to hide my teeth.

I met my best friend my freshman year. She also hated her teeth and body. In that and many other ways, we're almost identical. However, she didn't realize that she had the body I wished for! With her being insecure about **her** body, it made me even more insecure about **mine**. I would often compliment her and say, *"Your body is way better than mine! If you think your body is bad, imagine how bad I think mine is!"* I would always put her happiness before my own and lifted her spirit when she felt down. I knew there were a lot of things she went through that were far worse than anything I have ever been through or was going through. Me being negative about myself surely wouldn't have helped her problems. I always tried to keep her in her "happy place" because seeing her sad made me sad. Even her mom said that my best friend is more positive when she's around me. So, being with her and keeping her happy became my main focus.

There was, unfortunately, a price to pay for my sacrifice: *Being around her all the time made me feel less confident about myself.*

There was, however, a **fortunate** aspect to our relationship that took me a moment to grasp: **The more I was around her, the more I accepted the fact that I am the way I am — and it's for a reason!**

Either way, I had no choice but to start loving myself or nobody else ever will. I stopped saying that I was ugly and began replacing that "ugly" word with self-compliments…ones I would want someone else to tell me. The more I spoke them, the more I began to believe them. I also stopped seeing whatever other people and I thought was ugly about myself and started to see nothing but beauty. Soon, I gained back a little of my self-confidence, and my friend would try uplifting my spirit as well.

Not long after that change in me, I got into a relationship. In the beginning, he made me feel like nothing anyone else said mattered because he thought I was beautiful both inside and out. As time passed, more problems came along that we had to deal with. He then started to distance himself and acted like he was embarrassed by me. It was as if he was trying to hide the fact that we were a couple. That had me up at night thinking,

Turbulence of Self-Esteem

"Am I even good enough?" That Summer, he dumped me for another girl.

Even after that happened, I continued to not care about what others thought about me. My goal that Summer was to work on myself and my self-esteem. I started to wear clothes that fit my style better than what I wore before, which was just jeans and a graphic tee. When I walked into the school after Summer break, I **looked** how I wanted to **feel**. Wouldn't you know it? I started to get more compliments, and way more people wanted to talk to me, but I always kept my circle of friends small (I'm not the one for all the drama, so I stay out of its way as much as possible).

The best thing to do to help boost your confidence is to keep all positive people in your circle and remain positive yourself. Ignore the negativity people throw in your direction and **never** believe those things people say to you that you know aren't true. Lastly, and most importantly, **ALWAYS** stay true to yourself!

Tosha R. Dearbone

Turbulence of Self-Esteem

Latoya Christman

"My Four-Year-Old Self Needed Internal Healing"

Tosha R. Dearbone

For many years, I struggled with abandonment issues, rejection, fear, hurt, and pain as a result of being taken away from my parents at the age of four. It wasn't until I became an adult that I realized I dealt with low self-esteem. I found myself in and out of relationships, one after the other. Each one left me feeling lost and empty. I would meet men who were everything I did **NOT** want in a man, yet I was still attracted to them. I later learned that each man possessed certain characteristics of my biological father. I even compromised my self-worth by having sex before marriage — in some instances, unprotected.

The things I yearned for and needed were masked in denial, pride, and stubbornness. Knowing I had low self-esteem and dealt with some internal issues that only God could heal were just a *part* of my harsh reality.

I will never forget the time when I was 16 years old and went out on a date with a neighborhood friend who was 18 years old. I remember my mother having him come to the house and getting his license plate number and driver's license information—just in case anything happened to me. He was respectful and *appeared* to be a responsible person, so my parents allowed him to take me out.

I didn't know that on that night, he would try to take advantage of me...

I fought him with all my might as he tried to violate me. Eventually, I was able to jump out of his car with just my panties and shirt on, running down the street. I was so scared and couldn't believe he would try to do something so horrible to me. I called the police, and they took me to the police station

Turbulence of Self-Esteem

then called my parents. I didn't want to press charges against him or even let anyone know what happened mainly because his aunt was like a mentor to me. She and I hung out and attended the same church, so the thought of having to tell her would have been **devastating** and could have possibly ruined our relationship.

His uncles were well-known in the neighborhood, and my oldest brother knew him very well. I was afraid to let my brother know because I knew something terrible would happen. In no way did I want to put my family in jeopardy of being hurt or someone else getting hurt, for that matter. So, I grew up and kept my secret from people I knew. I never even saw him again until I was an adult. Once he laid eyes on me, he must have thought he had seen a ghost! He quickly jumped into his car and drove off. I thought, *"Wow! What a guilty conscious he must have!"*

Even after that incident, it didn't keep me from wanting to be in a relationship with someone. I had my "first love" experience at the age of 16. The soul tie the young man and I shared was so strong that when we broke up, I lost weight, my hair fell out, I couldn't eat, and my mind was racing with thoughts all about him. The relationship was toxic, and I didn't even realize it. I gave more of myself to him than he did to me. I never said much about it to him, though. I didn't understand at the time what it meant **NOT** to compromise my body just to show a man I "loved" him. At times, I felt as if I was obligated to sleep with the man I was with, even when I didn't feel like it.

When I think about those times now, I think it's crazy how I didn't honor my body or have the strength to walk away and speak up for myself.

Tosha R. Dearbone

Once I became an adult, I still didn't immediately recognize my self-worth. I married early, long before I knew what it meant to be a wife. I witnessed what being married *looked* like for 28 years, but didn't know all the work it took behind the scenes to maintain a **healthy** marriage. I was 26 years old, married, and a year later, had a baby. I didn't know that marriage was a *ministry*. All I knew was that he made me feel like I was on cloud nine. My heart was filled with warm and fuzzy feelings, and no one could tell me a thing! For the first time ever, I went against my mother. I told her I was in love and that he wanted to marry me. She said to me, *"Don't do it! You will regret it. It will bite you in the tail later!"* I didn't listen.

When I tell you that my marriage did **more** than kick me in the tail, I mean that it almost took me out of this world! I endured so much pain and suffering, it was ridiculous! I never thought one person could make me feel so empty and hurt. I was trying to process being a mother *and* going through a divorce. During that time, my dad who raised me dropped dead a month after I found out my ex-husband cheated and left me. I was literally a train wreck!

Now, I know a teen may think they are in love and that their parents have **no idea** how much the other person loves them — and yes, *to an extent*, that may be true. **However**, trust me when I say our parents have "been there and done that." They know when someone is not right for their child. As adults, we see things differently because we have been through it or have seen others go through it.

As a result of my choices, I endured so much unnecessary pain. It took years for me to get to a place of healing, wholeness, and learning to love myself. I went through some hiccups, in and out of relationships while trying to heal. Finally, at the age of 34, I decided to wait on **GOD**. One day, I asked God, *"Why am I not married?"* His response made my mouth drop to the floor:

*"You have been married all your life.
It's time to live a single life!"*

WOW, GOD!

Let me explain why God's words immediately put me in check.

Every man I had been with I treated **LIKE** a husband. I cooked, cleaned, had sex, and sacrificed my time and energy on those relationships, only to never get a return on my investment.

So, I decided to go through a season of consecration after accepting the call to ministry. During that time, God began to show me what I was dealing with and why I kept repeating the same cycles. God instructed me to "go back" to the beginning when I was a four-year-old child who had been abandoned and rejected. Apparently, I was still that four-year-old child who was walking around in a 34-year-old's body. I had yet to be healed from those pains of the past. I was distraught and cried for weeks until I asked God to heal and purge me from the pain of being abandoned by my parents.

Life will teach you many lessons, but if you listen to sound advice from experienced adults, it can and will save you from **a lot** of heartache and pain. I understand now that as a teen, I put myself in quite a few vulnerable and dangerous situations. Now, as an adult with a six-year-old daughter, I pray over her and am the best parent to her that I can be.

Tosha R. Dearbone

If I could go back and talk to my younger self, I would say to her, *"Listen to your gut, Latoya. If it doesn't sound or look right, don't do it. Don't be so easily peer pressured into joining a gang just to fit in. Stop being afraid to speak up for yourself, even if it will cost you relationships ending. Respect your body and, if you are not ready to have sex, don't do it. If someone violates you, speak up and tell someone. Pray more and seek out positive influences."*

It must be noted here that I wasn't a "bad child" or even one who was blatantly disobedient. I did, however, do some things I **knew** I shouldn't have done. I am blessed to have had a great set of parents who loved me unconditionally, never sheltered me, and provided me all of the essentials of life.

Today, I tell any teenager never to give up—even when a mistake is made.

I encourage **YOU** to do the following in the face of any adversity:

- ✓ Keep fighting!
- ✓ Never let anyone see you sweat!
- ✓ Place your feet on the ground every morning when you wake up and keep running the race!
- ✓ If you **ever** think about committing suicide, speak life over yourself—not death. Then, seek some help.

As a Life Coach for teens and women, I have learned that self-esteem and self-image play major roles in our lives. If they are not cultivated and nourished, a young woman will compromise her self-worth and dignity.

Turbulence of Self-Esteem

There will be many days when you feel like throwing in the towel and feel all alone. I promise you this one thing: **If you keep a constant and consistent relationship with God, He will sustain you.** I don't see myself as being any different than a lot of people. My story is actually one that you may be able to tell. The only difference is that God saved me in the midst of my drama and sinful ways—and He can do the same for you!

I pray my story has touched your life in a **major** way. I challenge you today to live and not die! Never compromise your self-worth, body, and dignity for **anyone**.

Go forth and be ***FABULOUS***, in Jesus' name!

Tosha R. Dearbone

Turbulence of Self-Esteem

Nykell Lee

"From Orphan to Heir"

Tosha R. Dearbone

Without a doubt, the most challenging time of my life began one month before my 15th birthday. My mother had suddenly passed away from a heart attack, and three months later, my father walked out of my life. Those two events shaped who I would become for years, as I battled with abandonment, trust, and rejection issues. The feelings of insecurity directly affected how I viewed myself as a teenage girl and a young adult.

To be honest, being asked to participate in this book project brought me to a head-on collision with feelings and emotions I had long ago buried—feelings of being orphaned.

On June 19, 1997, I woke up with puffy red eyes to a reality I hoped was a dream—a nightmare, even—but it wasn't. The person I was closest to in the world…the person whom I hadn't spent many days or nights away from (except for an occasional sleepover at a close family member or friend's house) was suddenly gone. There was an ache in my soul that remains indescribable to this day. I had never experienced anything like this before. In an instant, my entire life changed. I felt all alone.

For days after my mother's death, I laid in the bed and cried, not wanting to eat or talk to anyone. What could they say to bring me comfort? Truth be told, I wasn't just sad; I was angry with God! Time and time again, I questioned Him: *"Why did my mom have to go?"* I never received a response.

As the Summer went on, my dad and I worked to build a closer relationship. Up until my mother's passing, I would spend weekends at his house, but I wasn't as close to him as I was to my mom. For about two months, my dad would come to visit me almost daily. As we tried to rebuild our relationship, we discussed me moving in with him. One day after school, I expected to see my dad as usual, but without any warning or explanation, he was a no-show.

The next few days turned into weeks. The weeks turned into a month. I realized I was both motherless **and** fatherless. My dad had walked out of my life as quickly as my mom had died. I was already dealing with the constant battle of loneliness behind losing my mom; now, I had to struggle with abandonment and rejection issues as well.

While at school, I would overhear the other kids talking about what they did with their parents for the weekend, etc., and the feelings of loneliness would overtake me. I knew I would never have those moments again. I struggled to fit into a school that I was so proud and excited to tell my mom I was accepted into just the year before. There would be many homecoming dances, proms, talks about boys, and a graduation my mom wouldn't be there for.

Eventually, as time went on, I was able to start enjoying life as a teenager again. There were, however, times when I often found myself withdrawing from people because I didn't know how to manage the emotions I felt. Despite the adversities, I was still able to find a way to stay focused and make it to my graduation day. I know my mom was smiling down on me, proud because I hadn't let my circumstances get the best of me.

After high school, I decided to enroll in a college about an hour away from home. As I was getting my paperwork together for the school, I found out I needed to prove I didn't have anyone who would be responsible for my tuition. I needed to get a letter from the Social Security Administration stating I was eligible to file as an independent student on my financial aid application. After leaving the office building and opening the envelope, I saw the most hurtful and impactful word used to describe me—a word that spoke to the emotions I had felt since my mom died:

"ORPHAN."

I was an orphan!

Since I was determined to push forward and make something out of my life, I started college. Sadly, the same joy and excitement that my fellow freshmen had—the ones who were dropped off by their parents with all of the essentials they would need for living in the dorms—**THAT** joy was not felt by me. I didn't have anyone to tell me to study hard, be safe, have fun, or give me my goodbye hugs and kisses. Some days were harder than others, but somehow, I kept going. Just as I did in high school, I struggled through college to find my identity. I desired to be **anyone** other than the *orphan* I was labeled to be.

Quite honestly, it took me a few years to overcome the issues from my teenage years. The loss of my mom at such a pivotal time in my life caused me to struggle with my identity. Like many young girls tend to do in similar situations, due to my father's absence, I looked for love and validation from young men who couldn't provide those things for me.

Special Note: When you don't know your value, you will always sell yourself for cheap.

Turbulence of Self-Esteem

I believe my healing came by finally letting go of the anger and bitterness I held in my heart toward God. I sought His guidance and love for both healing and direction in my life.

As I continued to search for my place in life, my aunt invited me to her church one Sunday. The more I went, the more I found my place in the world. The more I prayed and studied God's Word, the more the weights of insecurity and my past I carried around for so many years started to lift off of my shoulders. I began to understand that although those bad situations had taken place in my life, God was always there making a way for me and that He had a plan for my life. Those unfortunate circumstances didn't define me as a person. I then came to embrace what the Bible says about me in Romans 8:28:

> "And we know that all things work together for good to them who love God, to them who are called according to His purpose."

There was a purpose in all of the pain I experienced! Without experiencing the love of God, I wouldn't have been able to forgive and reestablish a relationship with my dad before he passed away, something for which I am truly grateful.

Although my life didn't start joyfully, as if I had penned the script, it gave me the passion I now have to mentor and coach young people to be successful in life. I now have the opportunity to let others know that no matter how hard life may have been or may currently be, it can still turn out beautifully. The love I missed out on for so many years, I now get to share with my awesome son and the young men and young ladies who God sends my way to mentor.

There is no experience you can go through in life that you cannot get through. If you are experiencing a hurt, loss, or maybe even a trauma such as abuse, just know there is life on the other side. We were never promised an easy life, but life is worth living. Take it from the girl who had to basically raise herself from the age of 14 until now. Don't get me wrong: I've always had people in my life to help and guide me along the way. I have a great brother who was there from day one, and I have had mother figures who stepped in when my mom couldn't be there but sometimes, the anger and hurt got in the way, and I couldn't see it for what it truly was back then.

Something I have always been grateful for is that before my mom passed away, she embedded great life principles and love into me. She taught me to be strong and stand up for myself. When life tried to knock me down *(and sometimes, it truly did)*, I always got back up. There has always been something inside of me telling me that I can go on and not to give up. It is comforting to know I was never truly alone in this world. I know people say it often, but I really would not have made it without God being on my side. There were times when I didn't know how things were going to work out, but He always made a way.

The best and most sincere advice I can give to anyone who is struggling to make it through a difficult time or situation in life is to hold on and trust God. Trust that just like so many others and myself who have had difficult beginnings or middles to their life story, there is a plan for your life also. If you have a dream, hold onto that dream with everything in you. Let that dream carry you through life's ups and downs and bring you to where you are destined to be. Trust that there is greatness inside of you.

Turbulence of Self-Esteem

I tell my story not to make anyone feel sorry for me or to make it seem as if my life was worse than anyone else's. I tell the darkest and hardest part of my story to show you that you can overcome anything in life! Losing my mom is something I will never truly just "get over". There are many days when I miss her and still sometimes cry, but I know I am making her proud. I tell my story to hopefully inspire you to believe that no matter what life has thrown at you, you can knock it out the park!

I went from being an **orphan** at the age of 14 to now being an heir in God because Psalm 27:10 told me, *"...though my mother and father forsake me, the Lord will receive me."* I believe it, and so should you!

Tosha R. Dearbone

Turbulence of Self-Esteem

Tearini Hubert

"I am NOT What They Say I Am"

Tosha R. Dearbone

As I look back over the beginning of my teenage years, I realize that's when I was the most vulnerable and critical about my outer appearance.

I had to be no older than 13 years old and in middle school at the time (middle school didn't start until the 7th grade, depending on which school district you were in). I didn't know what to expect or how that time spent in middle school would change how I viewed myself as a whole.

The taunting started the first month of my 7th-grade year. Every day, I fought a battle within myself. I remember looking into the mirror, feeling ugly and being disgusted with myself—all because of what people said about me. It would be one thing if it were the same people teasing me, but the teasing came from different people who constantly pointed out how small I was *(as if I didn't already know I was an underweight 13-year-old girl)*. I recall being called all sorts of names, from Olive Oil to Popeye.

The verbal abuse didn't stop at school, though. I was also getting it at home as well. My parents never knew what I was going through at school because I wasn't the type to let my emotions show. I also wore my feelings on my shoulders because I was strong and wouldn't **dare** show anyone that I had moments of weakness.

One experience that broke me down like no other was when, on this particular day, I had just gotten my hair done. I was truly feeling myself! (You know how us girls feel when we just get our hair done, and it's slayed and laid!) Well, when I went to school, everyone told me how nice my hair looked…except for this one group of females who were older

Turbulence of Self-Esteem

and "more mature" than I was. This one particular chick (whose name I can't mention) who never liked me and always had something smart to say was the first to comment in front of everyone in the hallway. It was right before the 7th period when she said, *"She looks like a boney stick that doesn't have nobody's body with some nice hair. Don't no boy want no stick!"* All I heard was everyone's laughter fill and echo throughout the hallway. Even the "cute and popular" boys laughed at me.

I was so hurt and embarrassed! I could not figure out why that girl always chose **me** to insult. I went to my 7th-period class with tears forming in the corners of my eyes, threatening to fall. I thought to myself, *"I better not let one tear drop in front of these people! They can't see me cry. Nuh-uh.* **NO WAY!**" I managed to make it through the rest of the day without shedding a tear.

During the ride home on the school bus, I continued to keep all of that hurt and anger on the inside. As soon as the bus made it to my stop, I got off and **RAN** all the way home…with tears falling from my eyes. I rushed through the door while crying hysterically and ran straight into my daddy's arms. I clearly recall saying these exact words:

"Daddy, I can't ever gain weight!"

I never told anyone about what took place that day at school because I was too embarrassed to share.

As a result of my battle with insecurities within myself, I started hanging out with the wrong crowd of girls in school. Those girls were known as being "fast" and who "got around." Now, back then, I didn't know what those terms meant. I just wanted to fit in and be in the "in-crowd." I believed those girls were "it"!

Tosha R. Dearbone

Let me tell y'all something: **Reputation is everything.** If you start hanging out with a specific crowd of people, you will be labeled whatever they are—even if you aren't doing the same things they are doing. Lock the following sayings into your memory banks:

- *"You are who you hang around,"* and
- *"Birds of a feather flock together."*

You **WILL** be judged (especially in middle school) for hanging around the wrong crowd. Let me tell you this: **I WAS DEFINITELY JUDGED!**

At the time, I didn't even really know what sex was. All I knew was that those girls were known for doing it and because I hung around them, I adopted that same label of being promiscuous. I never had sex before, though! I was still a virgin!

It must be noted that my mama and daddy were strict. They didn't play that 'staying the night at people's houses' game. However, there was this **one particular girl** who my mama would always allow me to spend the night with—for whatever her reason.

Before I knew it, I started dressing like that girl (when I wasn't at home, of course). Then, I started acting like her. I would talk back to my parents and teachers and even talked about sex as if I had lost my virginity along the way (which I had yet to do up to that point). I would listen as she and her other friends talked about sex and desired to know how it actually felt. I believed I was ready to be "grown" like them. I wanted to be like them so bad, and I didn't know why!

Turbulence of Self-Esteem

Following behind the "in-crowd" caused me not to even know who I was anymore. My family and friends started telling me that I was changing and that they didn't even know me. It took me a while to realize that those girls were **NOT** my friends. They didn't care about me at all. Think about it like this: They were trying to get me hooked on the same things that they were doing! **FRIENDS** don't do stuff like that!

I needed to break free from all that was going on around me and learn who I truly was. So, as my 7th-grade year was coming to an end and the Summer was approaching, I stopped hanging out with most of those so-called friends. I realized that I, too, was labeled "promiscuous" and desperately wanted that title off of me. I knew that wasn't going to come easy.

I had to start believing in myself again. One day, I took a good look at myself in the mirror and said, *"I am **NOT** a whore! I am **NOT** a boney stick! I **AM** beautiful! I want **MORE** out of my life! I don't want to be like **THOSE** other girls! **I AM NOT WHAT THEY SAY I AM!**"*

According to the Merriam-Webster Dictionary, the clinical definition of 'self-esteem' is "a confidence and satisfaction in oneself." Studies show that there are teenage girls battling self-esteem issues every day, which is the #1 reason why suicide rates have gone up in recent years.

As I look back, I couldn't even begin to imagine what my level of self-esteem truly was. I didn't know my worth. I didn't recognize my value. I had no idea I was a **QUEEN** in the making at the time. Even though I knew right from wrong, I still did what I wanted to do because it made me feel superior and beautiful—not realizing that my reality would come to meet me face-to-face one day.

As I prepared to write this story, I read a book by Dorothy Parker called *The Complete Poems of Dorothy Parker*. Within, there was a quote that stuck out to me the most that said, *"In youth, it was a way I had, to do my best to please. And change, with every passing lad to suit his theories. But now I know the things I know and the things I do. And if you do not like me so, to hell, my love, with you."*

I didn't know then like I know now that the skinny, little girl from the Southwest side of Houston, Texas, who was labeled "promiscuous" would one day grow up to be a successful woman sharing her testimony with girls going through similar experiences. I was the type of person who always felt as if I had no one in my corner to turn and talk to when I felt like I didn't want to live another day on this Earth. I was consistently picked on by family members and people at school about my malnutrition weight.

Unlike I had available to me, there are many resources and support groups available that will help **YOU**, mentor **YOU**, talk to **YOU**, and encourage **YOU** to face your self-esteem battle hands-on; not run from it.

I shared my story with you to remind you of this one thing: **YOU ARE NOT WHAT THEY SAY YOU ARE!** You can become whatever you want to be and so much more, if only you believe in yourself and apply the necessary pressure to make it through to the next day…and then the next. Self-esteem literally begins with **YOU!** You have to know that no matter

Turbulence of Self-Esteem

what anyone says about you, you are not that person — unless you *choose* to be.

Speak **LIFE** into your precious existence because it is, indeed, precious! Know that you are worth more than the shameful words you speak over yourself. Embrace your flaws because they will become your best qualities if you want them to be. Use them for your good, not the bad that you may see them as at this moment.

Come on, QUEENS! Lift your head before your crown falls to the ground!

Smile, **QUEEN**! Smile! ☺

Conclusion

In closing, I want to first remind the co-authors of *Turbulence of Self-Esteem: A Young Ladies Journey* just how amazing they are! They combined their testimonies of past experiences and began to transform not only their lives but those of other young girls and women who may be in similar situations. These young ladies are overcomers!

In life, we aren't afforded the opportunity to pick and choose the experiences that we must face. In our case, our stories included sexual abuse, emotional abuse, physical abuse, spiritual abuse, and verbal abuse. Each instance could have possibly ended our lives...**BUT GOD!**

As a mother myself, I began to see life differently when I got pregnant at the age of sixteen. I knew some things weren't adding up in my life and chose to change the course of my journey. I wanted to be **FREE!** At the age of 16, I moved into my own home with my daughter (she was two months old at the time). If I didn't know anything else, I knew I wanted a *better* life for her than what I had experienced. I never want her to feel rejected, abandoned, overly emotional, isolated, or lacking in self-love.

The day I was introduced to Jesus and His love, it just felt right. Although I had yet to identify what I was feeling, a breath of fresh air entered me. I continued to seek God's face while piecing together a yearning for a close relationship with Him. Attending church every Sunday and reading His Word enabled me to mature in areas of my life I was unable to even

Turbulence of Self-Esteem

imagine before. What God said *to* and *about* me became all that I heard. I had to shut out the "noise" of the world so that I could begin loving myself.

As the years progressed, I learned that those unfortunate situations from my past served a higher purpose: God wanted to use me to help other young girls, young ladies, and women who looked like me. In 2014, I founded "Positive Express." The organization helps others recognize that **#SelfEsteemMatters**. The participants learn how to be transparent with themselves, undo or stop generational curses that have been imposed upon their identities, and the wisdom of God is increased in their lives. We emphasize that God created each of them in His image.

"And have put on the new self, which is being renewed in knowledge in the image of its Creator."
~ **Colossians 3:10** ~

Once that concept is embraced, one can't *help* but begin to see themselves differently. As a direct result, their actions will display Christ-like behaviors, and the transforming of their minds will be renewed with wisdom to ensure a successful life.

Without a doubt, you will always encounter bumps and bruises along life's journey. Adversity comes to **everyone** without exception. What differentiates **YOU** from *"them"* is how you posture while going through!

"Do not be conformed to this world, but be transformed by the renewal of your mind, that by testing, you may discern what is the will of God, what is good and acceptable and perfect."
~ **Romans 12:2** ~

On this journey called **"LIFE,"** know that you no longer have to hide behind the pain!

DECLARATION

Repeat the following daily:

I decree and declare that I no longer have to hide behind the pain. I can be a voice to speak up for others.

~ Tosha R. Dearbone ~

Turbulence of Self-Esteem

Questions and Quotes

1. If you were to describe your self-esteem right now, what would you say it consists of?

2. Why are you trying so hard to fit in, when you were created to stand out?

Turbulence of Self-Esteem

3. Why do you think God is taking you through troubled waters?

4. At the start of your day, what is something you can do to ensure the rest of your day is positive and productive?

Turbulence of Self-Esteem

5. Name five (5) things you love about yourself.

_____
_____
_____
_____
_____
_____
_____
_____
_____
_____
_____
_____
_____
_____
_____
_____
_____
_____
_____
_____
_____
_____

6. What would you consider is your biggest fear?

Turbulence of Self-Esteem

7. Ask yourself, *"What type of person do I want to become?"*

8. How do you overcome obstacles?

Turbulence of Self-Esteem

9. What makes you sad?

10. What makes you happy?

Quotes

"When you come to the end of the rope, tie a knot and hang on."
~ Franklin Roosevelt ~

~~~~~~~~~~

"Believe in yourself and all that you are. Know that there is something inside you that is greater than any obstacle."
~ Christian D. Larson ~

~~~~~~~~~~

"You should never view your challenges as a disadvantage. Instead, it's important for you to understand that your experience facing and overcoming adversity is actually one of your biggest advantages."

~ Michelle Obama ~

Appendix

Akita, L.G. (n.d.) Retrieved April 30, 2019, from https://www.goodreads.com/author/quotes/8297615.Lailah_Gifty_Akita

Edwards, J. Pastor. (n.d.) Retrieved April 30, 2019, from https://www.brainyquote.com/search_results?q=james+edwards

Hillary, E. (n.d.) Retrieved April 30, 2019, from https://www.brainyquote.com/authors/edmund_hillary

Larson, C.D. (n.d.) Retrieved April 30, 2019, from https://www.brainyquote.com/search_results?q=Christian+D.+Larson+

Obama, M. (n.d.) Retrieved April 30, 2019, from https://www.brainyquote.com/authors/michelle_obama

Parker, D. (2010). The Complete Poems of Dorothy Parker. Penguin Classics Group (USA).

Roosevelt, F. (n.d.) Retrieved April 30, 2019, from https://www.brainyquote.com/authors/franklin_d_roosevelt

Washington, M. (n.d.) Retrieved April 30, 2019, from https://www.goodreads.com/author/quotes/268402.Martha_Washington

www.ingramcontent.com/pod-product-compliance
Lightning Source LLC
Chambersburg PA
CBHW052151110526
44591CB00012B/1936